salmonpoetry
Diverse Voices from Ireland and the World

WE ARE AN ARCHIPELAGO

ERIN FORNOFF

Published in 2025 by
Salmon Poetry
Cliffs of Moher, County Clare, Ireland
Website: www.salmonpoetry.com
Email: info@salmonpoetry.com

Copyright © Erin Fornoff, 2025

ISBN 978-1-915022-84-4

All rights reserved. No part of this publication may be reproduced or transmitted in any form or by any means, electronic or mechanical, including photography, recording, or any information storage or retrieval system, without permission in writing from the publisher. The book is sold subject to the condition that it shall not, by way of trade or otherwise, be lent, resold or otherwise circulated without the publisher's prior consent in any form of binding or cover other than that in which it is published and without a similar condition, including this condition, being imposed on the subsequent purchaser.

Cover photograph by Bryan Derballa
Design & Typesetting: Siobhán Hutson Jeanotte

Printed in Ireland by Sprint Print

Salmon Poetry gratefully acknowledges the support of
The Arts Council / An Chomhairle Ealaíon

To Kathy Kelly

Who told me the story of Bill's going, and of his coming home.

Ocracoke is a small island about twenty miles off the coast of North Carolina in the United States, accessible by a two-hour car ferry. It was a pirate hideout for Blackbeard, who died on the island in 1710. Possibly, it was the last destination for the Lost Colony, a group of settlers who disappeared in 1580 – a mystery as yet unsolved.

The character of Bill is based on a real person. At the age of ninety-nine, he returned to live out his remaining days in his coastal homeplace. He passed away as he left the island for the final time.

Bill was tired of pretending the roar
of the highway was the sound of the sea.
This much land was unkind.
He wanted to taste salt when he breathed.

He left here at nineteen, but eighty years away can't revoke
the salt-scented memories of home. He came back to
wait to die here. She: knocked up, broke,
nearly crawled up the beach on her elbows – a cypher.
A potty-mouthed, shipwrecked, furious survivor.

The small effervescence of their company.
Him in the dusk of his days and her in the dawning,
the sadness that seemed to sit on their stoop,
just waiting to come in.

Deena felt water in her body, gradually swelling,
come to this island to bury herself. She doesn't know
love as anything but an insect that stings.

*

She can't speak a language that doesn't sing back in venom.

*

She'd find Bill's accent slowed, extra vowels
sagging the strings of his sentences.
She'd rag his tendency never to look right at her.
He'd startle at her staccato chatter,
words bursting forth like birds from under the eaves.

*

'I can't believe I've yoked myself to a Gen Z monster.'

His eyes on the line where the sea ends and the sky starts.

*'Well. I can't believe my only fucking friend
is a bag of rusty engine parts.'*

*

Ocracoke: this island, his holy land, her safe house.
No telling what fate had in mind
for the two of them (not yet three)
gathering like a pulled drawstring. Lonely.
His head and her belly full of brine.

Perhaps they'll find the roar of the sea becomes their highway.

*

Pirates once had a three-day party on that beach,
at the meeting of sea and land. Ask your nose
to conjure dark rum sloshed in sand and beneath it
the semen and sweat scent of the salt marsh.

The settlers came from Ulster in 1524,
Ocracoke, the sound like an axe chop,
this land a humid shock after the grey islands of home,
wind-rubbed and rocky.

*

I already feel I am part gone from this world.
They joke the old, when faced with the yoke
of technology, throw it off. It's not so complicated,
or unexplored, (I broke codes in the goddamn war.)
I just don't understand the solace they draw from it.
I'm sensitive about all I don't know,
like my not-knowing is endless.

The air here can mock you like a breath on a face,
the marsh like you're living in that mouth,
the pace of growth is mean: you'd be swallowed if you stood still.
And the cicadas, screaming like knives against a plate,
harsh and shrill.

Can we no longer imagine a journey with no turning back?
A trip irrevocable, and permanent, only onward, or death,
but not return. Those men stepped on a boat and sailed to the brink.
We'd take more careful strokes with ink.

I like to think of my trip here as one without a return ticket.
The inland place I fled squeezed me like a tourniquet.
But here – I can take my past and live in it.
Go back where I was born and watch the rest of my life pass.

Time turns coral into sand and lightning turns sand to glass.

*

'You sure don't speak like ladies do in the South.'

> *'Motherfucker, didn't you survive the Somme? You can handle my filthy-ass mouth.'*

'That battle was in 1916. How old do you think I am?'

> *'How old did you feel when you invented the goddamn wheel?'*

*

A journey with no turning back:
I thought the only one I had left in me was death.
I reckons I surprise myself with every breath,
every step on this path. I'm back on this island at last.
I am coral turned to sand. I'll see sand turned to glass.

*

*I'm too harsh with him. But I think it keeps him on his toes.
I can't trust his kindness isn't the kind that goes.*

'If I wasn't knocked up, you'd try and fuck me.'

He blushed. Looked anywhere but at me.

'Your grandmother would be too young for me.'

*

Imagine the first settlers stepping off that boat. At last.
The fear, that jungle, as it seemed to twist and writhe
before their eyes. That first night. The noise of the sea.
Cicadas on the boil in the canopy of foreign trees.

A neighbour helped him pack the house. Ninety-nine years of bric-a-brac.
A move should be a chance to shake things free,
but he's a packmouse. Poured his piles into stacked boxes.
Snailing it all on the ferry.

*

In a census a lone person is categorized a 'non-family.'

*

It is just me, on my own. Well, we. I'm on my own out here and she, in the single bedsit of my belly. Is she lonely? She's inside here. How isolating could that possibly be? Fuck, though. You can be lonely at a party.

I'm not running from any great legacy. I spent my shifts at the checkout wondering about the lives I was ringing up, beep – beep – beep – my grocery store career. Who is having a better evening? The guy buying a case of beer and one condom? Or the case of condoms and one beer?

After a while your soul starts this little creep –creep –creep.

I had to get out of there.

*

Jeremiah comes sometimes to micromanage me.
He'd walk in and move my TV to a 'better spot,'
never mind the shaft of light which bled the picture
dry from that angle. I have become old and
in his mind a child and something to be handled.

This island is a slash of wild at the edge of the Atlantic.
I come armed with memories, sepia nostalgic
for the kiss of the tide. For Oyster Creek.
Highway 12 snaked up Ocracoke's spine,
wild ponies fenced in by the boutiques.

Jeremiah calls me to critique me coming here.
It's judgement, but also fear. I love him,
 but I don't know how he got here.
My son is so hard – it is his flaw.
I don't know how I raised a child with claws.

*

I was struggling with a bag and he banged the screen door open to nag me. But he offered help, in this molasses tone. Mouthful of gravy. Accent from a movie. Me and my one bag and my big-ass bump. He'll want something. I'm a fucking chump. But it kind of felt like–she–beckoned him out to meet.

Only the tourists live on the beach. Bill had to teach me that. Locals are inland. Like, why would you cuddle right up with storms, when we're already praying every day? Here the salt eats wood, rust spreads before you know it. I set my ripped bag on the counter. Takeout flyers in a drawer below it.

I don't know how to do this. Be her mother. I've had no help. I know all parenting is on-the-job training or whatever, but I fucking raised myself. My home life was an afterschool special. My dad was negative space. Everywhere I stood I was in my mother's way.

*

This island once connected to its neighbour, Hatteras.
But fearsome storms swept away the sand.
A fickle breath of wind re-deposits the land like a promise,
connected them right up again.

*

No one tells you that old age makes your jokes adorable
instead of funny. I can't decide if that impulsive ride
on the ferry here is coming home or running.

Did I expect to cross the sound and see myself young again,
proud, exponential, loaded with potential like a weapon?

*

*Bad weather seemed a great reason to start drinking again,
to maybe buy a gun, to call a bad idea, invite him over,
blame it on the high winds. I did it to hurt myself, when push
comes to shove. I've never been a person that people love.*

*My stomach acknowledges what my mind still won't.
Drunken fumbling, a hangover, this high cost. I hid the blue
stick beneath the trash and gasped. Still numb, stumbling.
Carrying your simple fact.*

*I'll never tell this baby I tried to erase her smudge
I went to the clinic before I ever felt a nudge.
But that ship? Long sailed. Couldn't get within the window.
My reaction? I wailed. I'd soon be puking over the ferry bow.*

*She is a trip with no turning back. Permanent.
I am wordy and thus far, she is reticent.
But isn't she speaking in her own way, clear and elegant?*

*My mother emptied the trash and said,
that baby will be born a bastard. Ah, don't limit her, I said.
You never know. She could be born a dickhead.
I wanted to weep but I laughed instead.*

I will admit I watered denial with booze,
had a reflux of shame when I felt her move.
The guy showed up to pound my door, the window breaking
as I hid on the floor.

I lived in a ground floor flat by 1-95, New Jersey road roar
like the audience of some endless gig. I didn't know that
that concert din would soon be the ocean as trucks knocked
my cigs from the windowsill in their passing.

I took my belly like it was cargo, picked some small
nowhere down 95, with no one I'd known around. Make a
new me.

Figured I'd investigate the self-care properties of the sea.
(Am I the first unemployed shift worker with that luxury?)

I am sitting in this house with unfamiliar creaks
and groaning water in the pipes, salt air refreshing as fuck,
all this a secret just between me and her.
What if I'm not enough? What if she needs more?
When she moves it is half joy and half war.

*

The first time I heard a hail of curses like a scrape,
I slapped open the screen door a beat too late to help.
Her bag ripped and tore, scattered all the detritus of her day
on our shared porch. She swore.

I stepped out and attempted to stoop to the floor.

> *'Are you insane? Don't make me call an*
> *ambulance, you'll never get up, fuck –'*

It slipped out of me: 'You're not exactly equipped for lifting, all due respect.'

She smiled, almost. Held close like I'd steal everything she owned.

> *I thought he was the most fragile-looking*
> *man I had ever known.*

*

I asked her again, plain. From my door to hers:

'What's your name?'

        You can smell loneliness off a person like rain.

        Deena.

Now I knew one person on this island.

*

'I'm sorry, it's been a while since I talked to folks.
Can I help you with anything? No. I'll leave you alone.
I was born here, left for eighty years, then made a break –
figured salt would make my soul taste better. Like I'm a steak.'

> *His worry endeared him to me. That steak thing was funny. He wouldn't look at me.*
>
> *'So, you just came home to Ocracoke to die salty?'*

'Sandy. Die sandy. And apparently, I'm alive still.'

> *'Sorry, You still not helping with this fucking bag. What's your name?'*

'It's Bill.'

*

Now Bill is rounding ninety-nine and she is twenty-two and thirty weeks
and the days are slow and racing.
She is blooming like something southern facing.

*

Will he be to me, what a friend would be?

Did I come all the way back home to find a funny little family?

*

I taught him to text and his responses come twenty minutes later.
He signs them 'Sincerely,' and writes it like a letter.
I like being the expert, so yell next door to call him a luddite freak.

Is he becoming a familiar creak?

*I keep asking myself, is she really coming? Is this?
And her heartbeat answers,*

>*yes,*
>> *yes,*
>>> *yes.*

*I keep asking myself, where do I hide from all this fear?
And the waves answer,*

>*here,*
>> *here,*
>>> *here.*

*

I am a project for Jeremiah. He circles me like a sergeant,
berating. When you lose one you love you lose the person
 they brought out in you. I know Jeremiah suffers.
My wife could pull a sweetness from him I could never muster.

*

The first settlers to this area packed up and fled.
They carved this island's name on a tree.
We never knew whether they made it here –
their rescue ship was hurricane-driven out to sea.

*

I am informed Jeremiah's found a spot in a nursing home
and reserved it for me.

*

I notice myself waiting on the porch as the weeks pass. Slamming the screen door to let him know I'm here. I find friendships fraught, I don't trust anyone, but I just thought he needed looking after.

So far, I've just given him leftover lasagna.

*

She bangs that screen door and I don't want to come running,
these knees aren't built for speed anymore, they're humming with ache
and my body weighs a thousand tons – hell, more.
It takes me a while to get to the door. Longer to think of a reason.

I open the door and a grin briefly flashes and I marvel at how her face
blooms in seasons. A smile on her is the high note of an aria.

'I just came out to thank you for the lasagna.'

*

> *'Did you hear we've got a hurricane dropping right on us?'*
>
> *I said it calm but my heart had an uncanny lightness, like the feeling when I've smoked too many cigarettes and become a bit nauseous, unmoored from the floor. These days I don't feel light much, anymore.*

'What are you worried about?'

> *'Bitch, I just wanna know if I'll have to rescue your ass.'*
>
> *'So. New episode at 7:30?'*

She's gotten me into reality TV.

*

*I could hear him talking on the phone from
my kitchen, eavesdropping like a motherfucker.
I am attuned to tension when it's around,
know when something's about to go down
but it was more a low plead, a deflation.*

'Jeremiah, I will say to you again I am not going.'

'I know how old I am.'

'I am aware. I was there.'

'A non-refundable deposit? Oh, well then, in that case! Please, drop it. I came home to die home. Not in a nursing home.'

'What? Well, I'm not alone.'

'Where in all this overblown...I do not want any part of this.'

'I – I – I just – please.'

The phone call quits.

*

For a moment I sit.

'Bill!'

I finally shouted from my kitchen to his. He's quiet a minute. Finds shouting undignified and tactless.

'Yes?'

He acts a little annoyed but he's faking it.

'Where's the good beach?!'

'It's an island, it's all beach. Which one?'

'Best one!'

'Teach's Hole.

Would you like to go there?'

'Yes, I would, why thank you, what a great idea.'

*

No one seems to go to the beach unencumbered,
They lumber like snails with all their worldly possessions
in tote bag and basket. They unlatched two lawn chairs.
If you asked Deena if she was content, she'd deny it.
But a silence shared is a sweeter kind of quiet.

There was always something to him in the waves going
and going as the rose gold day waned around them,
the world going ever onward, gently crashing,
lost and found again, but it pained him too,
the weight of his nostalgia.
He half-expected all the old gang to be here on his arrival.

He thought all those characters in the play of his life
would be here waiting, breathing, ripe –
ever-present as the Gulfstream twelve miles offshore
but now this is a place he hasn't been before.
It's gone. They're gone. And he here, in some fluke, is left.

But the waves in the waning and the heft of the sand
and the marsh and the salt are the same. A relief.

She calls him back from his reverie.

*

'God, what is up with your feet?'

He chuckles good naturedly.
She is staring unabashedly.

'Do you cut your nails with a combine harvester?'

'Neither of us are up to much manicuring at this stage.'

He looks pointedly at her raggedy nails.
Her body in thrall to baby. His in thrall to age.

Deena's private wonder: was this kid the first thing she'd follow through? Bill's: the belief that he could choose when it was finally time to go.

*

The beach became a thing without making it so.
She'd slam the screen door and I'd meet her and in silence we'd go.
Sometimes we'd walk briefly, slow and unsteady,
She'd point at the shells she'd collect if she could bend down her hand.
I'd wait for her story to wash in on the sand.

*

'Father?'

I chanced it.

> *'Immaculate conception.'*
>
> *(Couldn't say 'kept calling the same one-night stand.')*

I wanted to say: I understand. And I promise delight can come to stay.

But I looked away.

Sometimes she withdraws for days.

*

*I left I-95 behind me like an unfurled ribbon
but all I left came with me, the gibbering waves
their voices calling me slut, poor, never amount
to anything, you cunt, you whore – I hid here
but they're here, and there's fucking more –
they're never through, my blood pumps
explosives I am a lit bomb, a furious boom you
will never hit me again FUCK YOU*

*

I saw her through the window, sitting on the kitchen floor
like her knees had torn their cartilage, holding her belly like a ball
rocking like her own little boat in a storm.

I couldn't go round there now.
Me knowing her in that kind of vulnerability –
She'd never forgive that witness.

I sat on my kitchen chair and listened. Stayed.
A heart can break for another heart a thousand ways.
I listened and revised a thousand approaches.
Dialed the phone for Little Italy. After the knock at the door,
I finally called across the porch:

'Deena? It appears – I accidentally ordered an extra pizza.
I'd be obliged if you'd come take a piece.
Deena. I don't have the fridge space.

Deena please.'

'Ok fine, Fuck it.'

*

She rose, the rocking and lurching the optimistic motion
of a nine months pregnant chick rising from the linoleum and padded
across the shared porch. They sat in silence, stringy drips from their lips,
as something in her eased. Turns out you can dry tears with hot crust
and cheese.

*

The baby kicks when I play music. When it first happened, I was floored. I'm nodding my head and baby's in there tapping on the two and the four.

So much dread with her coming – and then this joy surging almost against my will. I wanted to tell someone, then realised –

I could tell Bill.

Her music came bumping through the screen door
I didn't know it – but loved the cacophony of someone there.
I googled the lyrics. I was prepared.
Practiced my nonchalance secretly.

'Sorry, I can turn it down!'

'Oh, don't, I love Cardi-B.'

I laughed for days at the moment, her staring incredulously.

*

'It's due to hit land in the evening, tomorrow, 7:30.
We'll nail up the plywood and fill the baths, if you're free.'

> *I nodded. Watched too much news. Green sky already here.*
> *I'd kill for a smoke. Fuck. Cursed to push away the fear.*

*

The salt on the heavy air brought back forgotten storms of my boyhood.
The one that killed the four fishermen, the one that came brawling.
I remembered neighbours standing in standing water, weeping.
These days have already ripped the roof off me. All my secret keeping.

*

> *Cut to us pulling out plywood from the crawlspace.*
>
> *'I couldn't tie my shoelace if you paid me a thousand dollars. This roommate has taken up my full abdomen. I can't bend.'*

He widened his stance, angled down like a giraffe to lift the board.

> *'Motherfucker no, don't, please stop it, you're already nearly dead.'*

He hauls halfway up, rests with hands on bent knees, woozy, broken. His laugh rises like something just woken.

> *'OK, goddamnit, on three, lift it up to the sill.'*

'We are some scene.'

> *'Shut up, stay still.'*

She stretched to hammer the nails into the board.

'Hard to say which one of us is more vulnerable –'

> *'Or more ridiculous – the oldest man in the world or the knocked up future single mother. With our forces combined we have the strength of one normal motherfucker.'*

'Here, now – did I not lift up the plywood? Did you not get the nails through?'

> *'I can feel her kicking to the rhythm of music. I wanted to tell you.'*

*

They finished the windows as the light turned nauseated. It was weirdly green out. Inside Bill's house seemed haunted. Deena dawdled.

In this foreign currency of friendship she found she didn't even need to invite herself over, she wasn't used to that kind of given, she knew it was her space to go into.

*

A storm makes you feel small enough without two tandem solitudes.
I threw something frozen in the oven – figured we'd eat like kings
while we still had power. Various Italian leftovers had thus far been a
kind of sweet relief. She said she was coming on thirty-seven weeks.

The wind wasn't there yet but we could hear the moan coming.
Deena peeked out the door and saw the strip of sea foaming
like a mouthful of toothpaste. I told her to stop opening it
once she struggled to push it back against the gusts.
I could taste it in my fillings, something pushing my sinus.

The wind finally came and I could feel its fingers find us.
It fondled every inch of the house, prodding.
I turned the battery radio on. The lights blinked off.
Rectangles of light dimming around the plywood.

*

A lighter flicked like the start of an old record.
They moved to the living room, plotted a dozen small points of light.
Deena sat on the couch; Bill moved to the Laz-E-Boy through the
artificial night as the wind started to roar.

*

Just then – BAM BAM BAM.
I felt hurricane muscle memory – knew it was branches, debris

    It sounded uncanny like someone knocking

Suddenly Deena was huddled on the floor.

    Fuck me I've been here before, have I been here before.

    *

I stood, the rocking and lurching the optimistic prayer
of a ninety-nine-year-old trying to rise from an easy chair
and came over to sit on the far end of the couch while she sat
on the ground. She seemed to crouch. Unbound.

As best she could she wrapped her arms around her knees,
belly cradled and moon-full.

'I can't – That's a sound I already know.'

It struck me that on this island I had been coming
and she had been running – or trying to go.
The branches bashed the walls in the tempest.
I was anxious to fill the silence.

And in a contrivance that has never endeared people to me, I turned
to my secret weapon: history. She's scared?

I'll bore her with an endless lecture on the Lost Colony.

'The first settlers came to flee a famine on the other island around here.
Nobody knows what happened. They never found them.'

(I could go on like this an hour.)

'They may have joined the local tribe.
There's rumors about Native Americans with blue eyes.
Or maybe they died. Either way they went to ground.
I'm just saying it's not a bad island to go for not being found.'

        Deena's belly between her arms seemed impossibly round.

'There's a theatre show, on the next island over. Islanders play islanders
from that era, a band doing covers of its own tunes.
They cast the tannest ones as the Indians. Can you imagine?'

        'Sounds fun.'

'I beg your pardon. It's an overpriced abomination. Four hours under stadium lights in high summer. Battalions of mosquitoes feasting on you like a fine buffet dinner. You get picked the hell over.
And still never learn what happened.'

'Picked the "hell" over, eh? I've taught you well. The swear.'

'You've worn me down. I'm ninety-nine, you think I've never snuck a curse in there?'

'Did they all die, then? You're telling me there are a bunch of blue-eyed Indians?' Did they manage to flee here again?'

'Could be. Could be ancestors of me. The Lost Colony.
This place was so far afield Blackbeard buried his treasure here.'

She turned to him, interested as a child.

'So, Blackbeard buried his treasure here? That's wild. We should go look.'

'They never found that either. It took the better part of my childhood to case the joint for the X on the map.'

'Then I'm a pirate. A fugitive who adapted.'

'A pirate was someone who floats under no flag of protection. Entails no national obligation as well.'

'No fucking thank you, then. I've done that. It's lonely as hell.'

*

We heard an ugly melody I realized was water whining against the porch. Not knowing if it would, I said,

'It'll be fine.'

I sat on the far couch. She on the opposite side.

Do you miss your old life?

'My wife's been gone 24 years. It's abstract.'

'Was she the love of your life?'

'She was a good wife.'

'"A good wife." Fuck that sounds like no praise. Were you "a good husband*"?'*

'Sheesh. Lord, I don't know. On days.'

*

Jeremiah has been sending me tracts about the home.
They went straight in the trash.
The way you treat someone is often how they act –
I lose my facts. Jeremiah berates me like a sport.
The worst times, I saw him enjoy it.

*

My back hurt. The candle sputtered. I missed cigarettes. I was smoking when I came here, belly and all, the shame of Bill's witness the thing that pulled them from my lips.

I was so wary. But I thought him too frail to be an asshole.

He never mentioned the state of me. Never looked disapprovingly from my hand to my belly as I exhaled clouds into the night. I appreciated his slight discernment – like he knew I already knew. My man hated me, and I hated me too.

I will stand still forever if shoved.

I've always been a person who hid her love.

*

The wind shook the house like it sought to release it from its moorings. Low hums rose from both of them, unconscious. Then the wind went quiet. They were in the eye, eerie and silent.

*

What do you want?

I was so ready to hear the ugly answer, for his hand to drift. It was a fear I had always confirmed, sadly. Oh riiiight. Silly Deena. This is all they ever wanted from me.

I braced. Wary again. Built the wall in my mind.

And Bill – suddenly couldn't find words beneath the tears flooding forceful as a high tide. He blinked his eyes.

'I have forgotten everything that ever made me rejoice. I came here to wait to go.'

Worried it was a dumb comment.
Question had him thrown.

'You know, I won't be around much longer. I just wanted to come home.'

He was embarrassed to be so stuttered, so vulnerable.

'I'm sorry, I –'

'I want so much joy, joy starts to feel normal.'

She leaned her head back on the seat as he faltered.
High tide in his eyes again.

This must be what it's like to have a daughter.

She was still. Softened.

Who would I be if he'd been my father?

*

Bill stood in stages as the wind returned to groan.
She hauled herself up alone and moved to stretch on the couch,
She curled up under a blanket as he lifted up his footrest.

'I think the islanders came here and never left.'

He heard her muffled, saw drowsiness caress her face.

'I think they did, too. They made it their place.'

*

I slept on and off, would wake through bleary eyes to find him snoring in the chair, weary from the day. Probably weary from the years. I felt pressure in my belly and kept shifting. No lifting of the hips relieved it. Candles made the room soft amid the wind seething outside.

Next time I awoke I found myself soaked from the thighs.

*

'BILL. BILL!'

Is he fucking high?

'WAKE UP! It's time.'

My heart fluttered like a bird. Candles sputtered as they ran out of wick, and I felt a thick and thrashing cramp take over.

'BILL.'

I awoke and somehow knew before I had any cause to know.

> *'Please nooooo.*
>
> *Shit fuck motherfucker goddamn it cunting bastard fuck it –'*

'Stay there – you'll be alright.'

> *'Stay there? Like I'm going fucking anywhere –'*

She cried out again as her body cramped. Felt the pressure between her legs, hard and damp and some things made sense as she knew this primal need called push.

> *'It can't be happening in this fucking rush, oh my fucking God, Bill –'*

*

I moved quicker than I thought capable.
Once I rose, went to her and I paused before I touched her head.
She looked at me, begging like I had any answer.
And my only answer was: towels, water, holding her hand.

The wind making an unholy stand as it careened,
a heavy-breathing pissed off
chaos echoing inside the walls

But it wasn't chaos at all – I felt something overcome me. Suddenly the cells of my body seemed to have more knowledge than my brain, some wild choreography of muscles and organ, bone space and arch, swell and burst and riot – so far from daughter

It smelled like slaughter. It felt like some animal crouch,
cornered into carpet and couch. My own children seemed to come
gift wrapped, me sat in the lobby and informed after my wife
had combed her hair. This squall, Deena buffeted by her own cyclone,
felt like a foreign storm.

Breath like so many waves swarming against the retaining walls, the high foam flung caterwauling and then the head socketed into my pelvis and my thoughts became colours, I became simply a maker of sound, a splitting, and in some beginning my whole body roared wind-loud

and she was out

*

I held her, this sea-washed marvel, as I sat at the foot of the couch,
all blood and salt marsh and the small cry a tiny piccolo
rising over the bass drone groan of the storm.
Deena looked at me, and asked for her, soaked and owned
by this small conspiracy of wonder. She was leveled by awe.

Deena angled her below her heart for latching,
and in the sudden stillness of her feeding,

I found I could not stop weeping.

*

He had come to turn the last corner of his life on this sand.
Prepared himself to take this stand alone, among his memories. And he
had accepted loneliness like a given, his only friend his history.

But this, but this, but this: ambushed by friendship, and this impertinent
life he caught to take them from one to two to three.

*

I keep asking myself, where can you let go of all this fear?
And the waves answered,

    here,

        here,

            here.

I keep asking myself, amidst all of it, what is enough?
And three voices called back:

    us,

        us,

            us.

The furious darkness? It paled. A bright morning
leached the night's dark fury. The roiling winds?
Exhaled a perfect day over blighted beaches still churning.

He propped the door open to let the breeze into the dark house
at last. Deena lay on the couch.
She hadn't stopped mooning down into her arms.
And in the small doings that move things along, Bill was making breakfast.

A single car made it up the littered road. It was Jeremiah.
A knock came upon tired plywood.
The smell of life assaulted Jeremiah where he stood.
'Jesus Christ' – he saw the wadded towels, startled when he heard the cry.

He's come to get Bill, to the spot in the home, slot him back into his own life.
He started in on the questions, not aware it was not his right –
Bill and Deena facing sunrise, rising on their own tide.

*

On I-40, headed from sand to red clay to black inland peat,
Bill sits heavily in the passenger seat. He has salt on his mind.
He knows where the treasure is buried, of a funny gentle family
by the brown Atlantic, in a house built from shipwrecks.
His phone beeped. From Deena – a text.

'I couldn't fucking say it, but I love u.'

In place of the word she types the emoji red heart, the letter u.

He sits still. He starts, restarts –

'Dear Deena,' he types. 'I love you, too. Sincerely, Bill.'

There's this lump in their throats that's a sweet pain, gathering like a pulled drawstring. Him in the dusk of his days and her in the dawning, she finally fathomed the lesson: love could be soft and gentle, a blessing. And Bill couldn't bring himself just to watch the rest of his life pass.

He saw lightning turn sand into glass.

*

Deena leans on her porch swing before the panes of Bill's dark windows.
She looks down at her baby. She feels her fierce heart
cast something heavy away.

She decides to stay.

*

The land rolled past in the car, island quiet in Bill's rearview, glowing.
Jeremiah is talking but it's all just noise.
Bill's had enough life here to bracket a lifetime.
He opens his grip, and finally, finally,

finally

he goes.

*

The waves keep coming and coming,
as the light turns the gentlest rose gold.

*

Acknowledgements

Thank you to Salmon Poetry for taking a chance on a strange book, and to my dear friend Bryan Derballa for the cover photo. Thanks to Ruth McGowan and Bee Sparks at Dublin Fringe Festival for making space for me to try something new with the stage production of *We Are An Archipelago*, and to Johnny Taylor, Franziska Detrez, and Headfoot Collective for their huge contributions to the show. All gratitude to Carys Coburn, who met me for coffee to talk through this inchoate idea and then supported it through to completion – thank you for being a guide. Thank you to the Arts Council of Ireland for funding the creation of this work, to Kae Tempest for Brand New Ancients and endless inspiration from afar, and to Kevin Barry, Martin Dyar, Dave Tynan, Kerri Ni Dochartaigh, Colm Keegan, Felicia Olusanya, and Miranda Richmond Mouillot who read and fed back along the way. And thank you, most of all, to Bill.

ERIN FORNOFF hails from the Appalachian mountains of North Carolina and lives in County Clare. She has performed her poetry at dozens of festivals and events across Ireland, the US, and the UK including Glastonbury, national Irish tours including Ireland Is and Every Blooming Thing, and features on RTE and BBC. She performed *We Are an Archipelago* as a one-woman show at the Dublin Fringe Festival with 300kg of salt as a prop. Widely commissioned, she has also been published and anthologized in *The Irish Times*, *Winter Papers*, *The Stinging Fly*, *Cyphers*, *Architecture Ireland* and many others. Her first collection *Hymn to the Reckless* was nominated for the Strong/Shine Award. The recipient of Arts Council bursary and project awards, she served as the inaugural Writer in Residence for Ireland's Inland Waterways for 2022. She is currently completing her first novel.

salmonpoetry
Cliffs of Moher, County Clare, Ireland

"Publishing the finest Irish and international literature."
Michael D. Higgins, President of Ireland